NEW DAY

Cecily Crossman

ISBN 978-1-7353091-0-1

Illustrator:
Mary Eleanor Hurt

Special acknowledgment:
Thank you to Renee Ellis for recreating
the illustrations for this book.

Interior and Cover Layout & Design:
Tarsha L. Campbell

Published by:
DOMINIONHOUSE Publishing & Design, LLC
P.O. Box 681938 | Orlando, Florida 32868 | 407.703.4800
www.mydominionhouse.com

The Lord gave the Word: great was the company
of those who published it. (Psalms 68:11)

Dedication

This book is dedicated to my children, my grandchildren, my great-grandchildren, and all the generations to come.

THE AWAKENING

I'm not the person I'm going to be,
But I'm getting to be.
Getting Free

"Cecily Crossman's poetry is sharp, cutting, fresh, and full of surprises. The poems are rich with amazing life-experiences, reflecting a woman blessed with a keen wit and deep faith. The spiritual truths therein entertain and delight.

I can only the imagine the inner challenges Cecily faced in the noble and often confining roles of mother and minister's wife. She shares her inner challenges so fully, with intelligence and laugh-out-loud humor. I love her poetry and saw pieces of myself in her stories. Her positive spirit uplifts and inspires."

Rachel Allen, Director | Peace and Justice Institute
Valencia College

"It's been said that empathy strikes at the gut but compassion strikes the heart and requires action. These poems strike at the heart and compel us to act on behalf of others."

Dick Batchelor, Former member of
Florida House of Representatives and Founder of
Dick Batchelor Management Group, Inc.

"This collection of poems written by Cecily Crossman is thoughtful and provocative. Each poem leaves a lasting impression and paints a vivid picture of Ms. Crossman's view of substantive and serious issues. The title of each poem is inviting and aids in the understanding of her thought process. Insightfully written, it is amazing to learn that most of these words were penned more than 40 years ago. It was a joy to read this wonderful book of poems!"

Dr. LaVon W. Bracy, Author, Co-Founder of
New Covenant Baptist Church of Orlando

"Cecily's book of poems is a witty tribute to marriage, family, friendship, and love. Her reflections of what it is like to be a wife, mother and friend are as relevant today as when she first wrote them forty years ago. With humor and grace she addresses the very real feminine struggle to be valued as an individual while also serving as someone else's wife and mother. She offers an honest and sentimental glimpse into her own remarkable life that creates an instant connection with her readers."

Stacey Dickenson Cox, Director of
Events and Sponsorships, Winter Park, Florida

"Cecily Crossman first published her book of poems 42 years ago and they are as fitting and timely in 2020 as they were in the 70s. What a treasure for her family and generations to come. New Day will leave you thinking about family dynamics, the evolving role of women in the workplace and social justice. But there are also moments that a poem will leave you chuckling and in some cases laughing out loud. Cecily has poured her heart into this gem to share with her family and the rest of us."

Vanessa Echols, News Anchor | Host of Colorblind:
Race Across Generations

"Cecily has spend her life coaching and inspiring others to change the world both as a consultant and as a mother. *New Day* gives us a window to know more of her heart and mind."

Pamela C. Kancher, Executive Director
Holocaust Memorial Resource and Education Center of FL

"I write to commend Mrs. Crossman on the beautiful book of poetry. I have heard it stated, although I do not know the source, that poetry can sear your soul. In this volume of her works, I found that to be a true statement. These poems were profound in simplicity of language that calls upon the reader to fill in with context of their personal situations. I found inspiration to explore memories from my days of motherhood to a young son, encounters with difficult people, and the joy and wonder in nature and relationships of all types.

The poetry evokes a depth of emotion that is refreshing, although it probes at deeper sensibilities and perspectives. The use of humor creates a welcoming envelope for reflection. In fact, I found that I wanted to absorb many of the poems several times. In each reading, I discovered a nuance that was new from my previous read. This volume is the type of work that can be reread many times and still offer a dynamic exploration of matters of the heart.

The author's heart is reflected in these works, and it makes me long to know her individually. Although it is not possible to establish that friendship now, I have the joy of experiencing her heart for family, faith, and respect for individuality in her works. I plan to use these works for inspiration and solace, and heartily recommend it for others to do the same."

Anne B. Kerr, Ph.D,
President of Florida Southern College

"Cecily's heart, humor and wisdom are on full display in *New Day*. It is an encouragement and inspiration during challenging times."

Samantha O'Lenick, Executive Director,
Community Impact, AdventHealth

Now all we need is to continue to speak the truth fearlessly, and we shall add to our numbers those who will turn the scale to the side of equal and full justice in all things.

- Lucy Stone, 1818-1893, Abolitionist and Suffragette

One of the reasons I like poetry is because it tells the truth while using only a carefully selected brevity of words. Great poets like Robert Frost, Emily Dickinson and later on, Maya Angelou and Mary Oliver told the unvarnished, sometimes hard to swallow truth as they experienced it.

Mary Oliver's famous work, "The Only Life You Can Save," is a poem of transformation. Likewise, the poems in this book, written decades ago, were, for me, a chronicle of my own personal transformation.

Do not confirm to the pattern of this world, but be transformed by the renewing of your mind. - Romans 12:2a

- Cecily Crossman

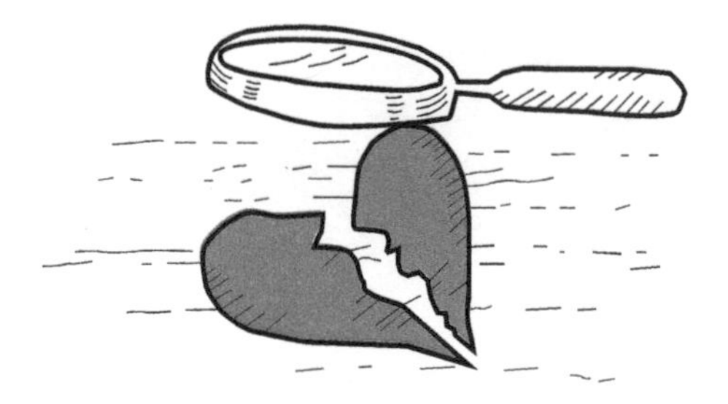

HELP STOP CRIME

I accused you of a felony,
I thought you broke my heart,
And ruined my life,
But,
After thoroughly investigating
the crime,
I will concede,
It could have been an inside job.

BEWARE OF TODDLERS

He is learning to walk.
A stiff legged,
Top heavy,
Chubby body.
Trying to stay erect
As he,
With one fell swoop,
Removes all the articles from
    the coffee table

As I lovingly watch,
I realize he is not unlike
Frankenstein's Monster.

RAMIFICATIONS OF STATIC CLING

As he stood up to ask,
The mayor's wife to dance.

A little baby sock,
Fell from the leg of his pants.

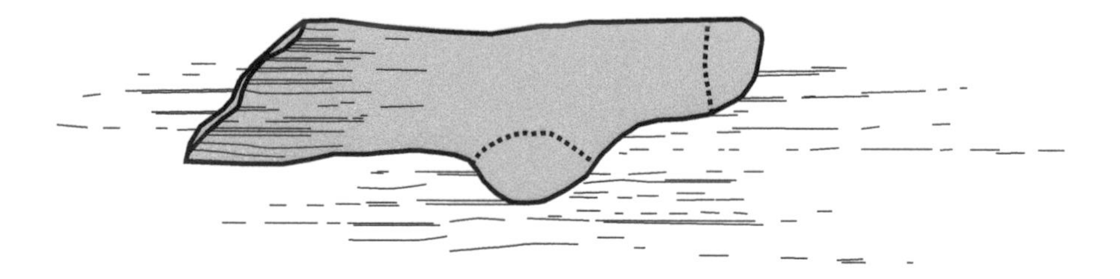

IS EGGS OKAY?

Remember the awful meals the
    children used to fix?

One birthday morning I awoke to a
    laborously crayoned sign,
On my mirror saying,
"What do you want to eat?

A banner in the hallway,
Confirmed my worst fears,
Saying,
"Is Eggs Okay?"

It's only now,
After several years rest,
That I can honestly say,
Yes, Scott,
They is.

DAVIE

In Davie, Florida
There is a huge mausoleum
Shaped kind of like a pyramid,
But looking remarkably like
    a pencil,
Jetting out of the ground toward
    the sky.
(Is there an eraser sinking
    in China?)

When it comes to it's full
    height,
Will it write a message in the
    clouds?

What will it say?

____

____

____

MR. BIG

I came through his door,
Bursting with ideas, dreams and plans,
Unaware,
That I was one of hundreds of women,
Who had come through his door,
Bursting,
Only to be met with apathy and boredom,
A dullness behind the eyes,
That had grown over the years into an
    automatic response.

I finally admitted to myself,
Once more,
That I had met another one of those men,
Who could advantagiously be,
Replaced by a computer.

Not just in his job,
But in everything he does.

Just picture it!

P.S.
It's not good enough anymore, Mr. B.,
We're on to you.

THE TEN YEAR PUNCH LINE

I bragged to you,
That an old time cowboy star,
Was related to me,
And you said,
"I don't believe that he is your
relative."

We went to a family reunion,
And you met his sister and mother,
But when we came home
you said,
"I don't believe that he is your
relative."

One evening,
The paper said,
"Old Time Western Star Found Drunk
and Disorderly"
And you said,
"I see where your relative is in
trouble!"

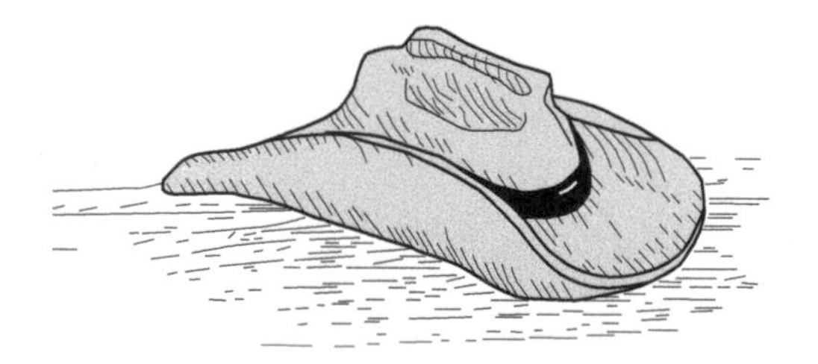

DEAR PAUL

Dear Paul,

When we were young,
I knew you well,
The sensitive little boy,
With flashing brown eyes.
Silly but shy,
Brave but afraid,
At times you were my whole
world,
And there was pain in not
being able to protect you.

You were building walls even
then,
And it was hard to break through,
But there was so much there,
If someone had only taken the time.

We've grown up now,
And I don't know you anymore,
Sad,
But that is the way sometimes,
With brothers and sisters.

But I still know that little boy,
For God, in his astonishing way,
Has given me another chance with him,
For, you see,
He is my son.

THE PERFECT ALIBI CONTINUED

You were hours late for dinner
    again,
The egg rolls I had worked on,
All afternoon were limp,
Contrasting my rigid demeanor.

Our dinner guest,
A psychiatrist,
Seemed bemused,
And appeared to be,
Mentally taking notes,
On the unfolding of this,
All too frequent,
Domestic drama.

I remained calm,
Throughout the description,
Of your last minute gallant efforts
To save a public official's job.

But the part about rescuing,
The man trapped in the revolving door,
Was just too much!

Why can't you ever,
Just stop off,
For a few drinks,
Like a normal person?

THIS AREA FOR AUTHORIZED PERSONNEL ONLY

Sarah, who is five,
Is into drawing houses,
She comes home every day,
With three or four pictures,
Drawn of tall houses,
With peaked roofs,
They always look the same,
With a giant window in front,
And a door with an outsized knob.

I wish I could climb into her mind,
To find out what she's saying,
But, I guess that would be trespassing.

MARGARET RITZ

Margaret Ritz, Margaret Ritz,
I'll call you when I can.
You haven't seen me lately,
But that was the risk you ran,
When you chose me for a friend,
And cluttered up my plan.
I do important things, you know,
I'll call you when I can.

Margaret Ritz, Margaret Ritz,
I heard you when you said,
That friends are hard to come by,
But I've got to plan ahead.
Now you've played an awful trick on me,
In the church Bulletin I read,
While meditating on my life,
"Margaret Ritz is dead."

HARRY - REMEMBERED

Harry was beautiful,
With black glistening hair,
Handsome, laughing face,
And magnetic eyes.

Harry loved,
People,
Expensive cars,
Fine clothes,
and life.

I loved Harry
He was irresponsible,
Flamboyant,
A magnificent personality.

One day a letter came.
"Harry is dead."
I cried,
Not for me, but for Harry,
Who had within himself a special treasure.
But never found the key.

THE HUSBAND IS IN / OUT

Catherine sits waiting,
As she has before,
Facing the new day with doubt,
Wanting to share the loneliness,
But for her, the Doctor is OUT.

He's saving a life,
He's saving the world,
He's treating the Mayor for the gout,
But Catherine must deal with her life
by herself,
But for her, the Doctor is OUT.

He runs to her,
When he needs shoring up,
To rethink what life's all about,
But Catherine has absolutely no place to
turn,
For her, the Doctor is OUT.

LIZZY STEPS OUT

(To Be Chanted)

Look out Lizzy,
Your world's falling down,
He says he's leaving,
For a new love he's found,
I know you've been married,
for 21 years,
You've begged and pleaded,
And shed lots of tears,
But he thinks you're boring.
And placid and dull,
With just no life of your own,
At all,
And even though the life
    you've lived through,
Has been his,
It doesn't count,
He wants out,
He's leaving.

Well, he's been gone now,
For 34 days,
And you're still seeing life,
Through a tranquilizer haze,
Come on, Lizzy, don't give up,
There's a world out there,
Go fill your cup,

But it's hard to see yourself,
As anything but "wife,"
When for 21 years,
You've lived another person's life,
But that's all over,
It's through,
He's gone,

(continued)

Come on Lizzy
Let's celebrate living,
You're accepting too much,
You need to be giving,
You're a person of worth,
You're a giver of love,
There are things to be done,
That you've never dreamed of.
Don't think about him,
It's over
He's gone.

Hurray for Lizzy,
She's on the right track,
It's been two years now,
And she's not looking back,
She's making decisions,
She's dealing with "what is,"
(Remember when all of the policy-making,
was his),
Life is different,
That you can't ignore,
But you found out something,
You might never have known before,
About you,
You're complete,
You're whole,
And that's enough!
(For right now.)

SIGNS OF THE SEVENTIES

I feel like I'm caught
In mid stream changing horses,
Acknowledging priests' weddings,
And ministers' divorces.

ROSA

The policewoman called
And said Rosa was in jail again.

She said,
"Can you help her?
It's her special problem
That makes her do these things."

Rosa's special problem
Is that her boyfriend cut off
Her nose in a fight.

She wears a bandaid
Across the center of her face.

When I explained this to you,
You said that was no reason
For Rosa to sell her body
And get drunk all the time.

Lady, how would you know,
You have a nose!

LIFE STORY

We met in Chicago, in the spring,
And I was wearing a navy coat (remember the
one with the funny buttons and the big loops?)
And we fell in love that day.

We married in the little church in the park,
And the world was bright and warm and clear,
And I thought,
"There must be a God somewhere looking down on us."

In the years that followed, (there must have been
bad times but I remember only the adventures)
You loved me and you were my strength,
And I began to know,
"Yes, there really is a God".

The children were born - and grew,
And our love took on new meaning - new scope -
new dimension,
And I wanted to shout to the world,
"There is a God who loves us all!"

Then they were gone, (it seems we had them such a
short time)
And we settled back to living in each other,
And I said,
"God is good."

Then one day you were gone - just like that -
you were gone.
I am alone now.
The pain is unbearable and yet there is no alternative
I am confused.
Is there a God?
Where is He?

THE COMPLIMENT

He told you (in order to help you to
 understand me as friends often
 tend to do).
That he considered me,
A "dominant woman".

Thanks for not telling him the truth,
That I'm a fool for you,
(I thought everybody knew!)

He explained to you,
That "dominant women" just have to
 have their own way in their personal
 lives or they become very frustrated.

Dear one, thanks for not telling him,
That you named all of the children,
(That I had the last two just to please you),
That my joy comes from wrapping my world
 around you,
That I'm a fool for you,
(I thought everybody knew!)

He told you,
That you would trouble with me later
 on because "dominant women" are not
 content to stand in the shadows.

Love, thanks for not letting him know,
That, to me, basking in your shadow is
 heavy stuff indeed.
It's not that I want to be a push-over,
I just can't help it,
I'm a fool for you
(I thought just everybody knew!)

DEAR JOHN

Dear John,

Remember when you were 18 months old,
And you poured a half gallon of
Wesson Oil on the carpet,
And that same day,
You upended the wastebasket into
your bath water?

You were the last,
Our unplanned one,
And, at times, I wanted so much to
escape.

Maybe go to work,
Eight hours in a salt mine,
Would have been a breeze,
Compared to some of my days at home
with you.

I'm so happy I stuck it out.
Are you?

DEAR LORD

Dear Lord,
  She asked me if she could powder her
    baby and I absentmindedly said yes.

  When I got to her room,
  She had powdered,
  The walls,
  The carpet,
  The fish tank
  The bed,

  And the poor baby John,
  Was white from head to toe,
  With only her round brown eyes,
  Sparkling through,

  Thank you for a sense of humor.

LORD

Lord,

I sure could use some glamour in my life.

This morning,
While he was doing his number,
(And doing it very well),
At the city commission meeting,
I was scrubbing down the kitchen walls.

And wishing I was flying off,
In some jet somewhere,
For a romantic weekend,
Surrounded by witty, interesting people.

And then I changed the baby's diaper,
And found,
Four pieces of Play Dough
And a little rubber tire.

Lord,
I know I must stay here and tend to this,
But I sure could use some glamour in my life.

SHATTERED DREAMS

The Sears catalogue,
Had a picture,
In the Linen section,
Of a beautiful lady,
Lying in her bed,
On Sears sheets,
With her arm around,
A beautiful baby,
Lying beside her,
You've seen the picture,
Haven't you?
My baby never laid,
In my arms,
On my bed,
On the Sears sheets,
He usually cried,
Or threw up,
Or worse,
Or tried to crawl into the
Bookcase in the headboard.

The Sears catalogue,
Had a picture,
In the furniture section,
Of a beautiful lady,
Sitting in an Early American
rocker,
With her arms around
A beautiful child,
Sitting on her lap.
You've seen the picture,
Haven't you?
My child never sat,
In my arms,
In the rocker,
On my lap,
He usually cried,
Or sat on the
Arm of the chair,
And took us on a,
Death defying rocker ride.

Why doesn't Sears tell the truth?

HAPPY BIRTHDAY TO YOU
YOU LIVE IN A ZOO

Happy birthday, darling,
Here's to the full life you'll live,
It's time for your lesson in ripping off,
Your family,
Every friend,
And relative.

Never mind the joy of having,
People who love you around,
"Just keep those cards and presents
coming in,"
You can measure their love by the pound.

Be sure mommy has a big party,
And invites friends and enemies alike,
And maybe she'll hire a clown this time,
Or a monkey who rides on a bike.

Remind her, her reputation's at stake,
If she "cops out" she'll look like a leech,
Can she top Georgie Brewster's party last
month,
With the helicopter rides to the beach?

I know that they've taught you in Sunday
School,
That love and charity are real,
But it's time that you learned the truth
dear child,
All of life is Let's Make a Deal.

BAD ADVICE

She said,
Wouldn't you like to have another child,
To replace the one you lost?

Replace the one we lost?
I can replace my Singer sewing machine,
And my Rogers Brothers Silverplate,
And possibly my victorian rocker.

I cannot replace Margaret,
Children are not interchangeable,
They come "one of a kind."

I AIN'T THERE YET

I can successfully pull off
a dinner party for a dozen VIP's
on a 24 hour notice
but
I am totally and completely
intimidated by
Hairdressers
Salespeople
Gynecologists
Most Ministers
Strange women who try to kiss me
Strange men who try to kiss me
And anybody who calls me "Honey".

INFORMATION I WISH I DIDN'T HAVE

Part of Adolf Hitler's
personality problem
was due to
poor potty training

REINCARNATION

The little things you do
Have such a profound effect
On my being
That it seems certain
Our lives have touched
In generations past.

Ah, but here's the rub
I didn't like you then,
either.

SHE SAID TO ME

She said to me,

"My dear,
You are smart to stay at home
with your little ones. After
all, it is such a short time
from birth to the time they
start to school, it's really
no sacrifice."

"Listen Lady,
From the time my first babe
was born until my last starts
to school, I will have 'stayed
at home' for 17 years."

That is a longer sentence than most people
get for man-slaughter.

WHY WOMEN'S LIB CONFUSES ME

Am I the cause of all
my problems,
Or is he?

MOVING DAY

I'm tired,

Of not having anything
That I've had for a long time,

Of having each child,
Conceived in a different bed.

No,
I won't go.

THE HAND-ME-UP

All big families have hand-me-downs,
But we have a friend,
Who goes to truck showings,
And buys elegant little dresses,
For her elegant little daughter,
And when they are out grown,
But still like brand new,
She gives them to us,
For our elegant little daughter.

And we can almost hear people say,
As we descend on a scene en masse,
"Isn't that nice,
A well-to-do girl,
Has adopted a poor family".

FORGET IT

When I am confessing to you,
That life is getting me down,
A little bit,
Please don't tell me,
About the parapalegic you know,
Who is always cheerful,
Or the mother of three retarded
    children,
Who never complains,
Or the heroine addict,
Who has "gotten it all together,"
Through sheer self determination.

It only makes me feel guilty,
And that's not what I need.

MY AUNT

My Aunt in Spokane
Wrote me again,

"Did you get the shawl
I knitted you dear?"
Which translated means,
"Why haven't you written!"
The reason is,
I don't know what to say.
I wish I had in my possession,
A paper entitled
Acceptable Things to Write to Your
    Relatives

My aunt in Spokane,
Wrote me again.

"Is your family sick?
Are you working too hard?"
Which translated means,
"Why haven't you written?"
She thinks I'm different.
The one who writes those
    odd poems,
And has the husband,
With the strange occupation,
(What does he do for a living
    anyway?)

(continued)

My aunt in Spokane
Wrote me again.

My cousin, the one in the family,
Who really made it,
Is with the F.B.I.
I've often fantasized
That he entertains at family reunions,
By reading aloud my dossier.
The scariest thing about that is,
It would be so frightfully dull!

My aunt in Spokane,
Wrote me again.

Why do I need her approval,
When my real family
Has accepted me
Just like I am.

I don't know why
But I do.

OF COURSE I LOVE THEM
I WOULD EVEN LIKE MY SISTER TO MARRY ONE

I have some practically perfect
    friends,
They love me just like I am,
They're the people I like to have
    around,
Whenever I'm in a jam.

They're at peace with themselves,
They've found their niche,
But most of all
THEY'RE VERY RICH!

In fact, their greatest problem seems
    to be,
That they find themselves stuck with
    friends like me.

I seem to have the need,
When we're gathering for tea,
To say something stupid,
Like, "how is your money?"
(The same principle here would apply,
If you met S. Davis, Jr. and said,
"How is your eye?")

Yet they seem to love me,
(Even when the blundering goes
    farther),
And seem to be immune to the envy
    I harbor,
(I wonder if, in their place, I would
    bother.)

Oh, one of the burdens of the rich
seems to be,
To patiently put up with people like
    me.

SEYMOUR AND SMOUSE

Did you ever,
Know somebody,
Who consistently went about saving
        your life,
And try as you might,
There was no way to get even,
Or simply express an adequate thanks.

So you
(Even though you were tempted to
        resent this one sided deal)
Finally grew in grace enough
To accept it,
And went about trying to act like
The saved life was worth it.

And in the unfolding of all this,
You caught a little glimpse of God?

Did you ever?

MR.LaGRAND THE FAMOUS MAN

As I stepped off the train in Winterville and trudged up the lane
to the center of town,
The soot from the paper mill high on the hill made the two-day
old snow all crusty and brown.
On the porch of the Winterville Hotel, three old men huddled
in a tight little clan,
And it was hard to believe as I looked all around, that this was
the home of the "famous man."
Shortly, farther up the lane, there loomed a large house where
the gray mist had been,
And I could not help but wonder, as I trodded along, just what
secrets it held within.

II

The home was comfortable, with a large, snow covered lawn,
And Mrs. LaGrand was charming, though withered and drawn.
After a coffee and rolls - and according to plan -
I asked the inevitable question, "What is it like to be married
to the 'famous man?'"
And she said with a slightly whimsical sign,
"Perhaps the children could tell you better than I."
In complete surprise, I exclaimed, "Good Heavens!"
And she said, "Didn't he tell you about them? - We have seven!"

III

"Margaret was born in '38
While he was born in Philadelphia for a labor debate.
And then two years later while he was in Rome,
I brought our first son, Jonathan, home.
When David had polio we needed him about,
But that was the summer his first book came out."

IV

"Catherine had a lovely wedding with a gown that swirled to the
floor,
But he had to be in Saigon at the time - something to do with the
war.
The twins resented their father at times, and the role they
believed he'd shirked.
But they just didn't understand what motivated him and the
importance of his work."

V

"On the night my husband received the St. Regis Medal for
Humanitary Service,
Our daughter, Julia, swallowed a bottle of sleeping pills in
a hotel room in St. Louis.
She muttered something about a man as they tried to bring her
about,
But, if course, her father made certain that the newspapers
didn't find out.
Oh, we realize he's too busy to bow to our little whims,
And in many ways we know we've been a disappointment to
him."

VI

The next morning Mrs. LaGrand drove me to the train,
Past the paper mill and the Winterville hotel - down the frozen,
snow-packed lane.
As I entered the station I looked back and saw a lady approach
Mrs. LaGrand,
And as the train pulled away I heard her say, "How fortunate
you are to be the wife of such a famous man."

STEREOTYPING

I have a friend,
One of those people,
You think of as,
  a good wife and mother,
Quiet, loving and home bound.

One day I needed help,
In an important job,
She volunteered,
I was dubious,
She was magnificent!

"What did you do before you became,
  A GOOD WIFE AND MOTHER."
I asked,
(Naturally, I had assumed she was
  born that way).
"I was an assistant professor at
  Georgetown University,"
She said.

And I said,
"Why doesn't anybody around here
  know that?"

She smiled and said,
"They never asked."

SURFACE FRIEND

She appeared at the door,
With her children,
To spend the day
Because she had heard me say
That I was lonely.

"Lady, you don't understand."

I am lonely because
The earth is such a small plant
In the universe,

Because 20,000 people died
In the Guatemalan earthquake,

Because I am a middle aged,
Motherless child.

I thought everybody felt that way,
Sometimes.
Don't you?"

HEADACHE #34

I was mingling at the party
Like we're all supposed to
When somebody asked the old
Mind boggling question
"What do you do?"

As usual,
I froze.

Through my mind flashed
Writing . . . teaching . . . sitting
on boards . . . demanding justice
for powerless people . . . working
on the thesis . . . working at the
hospital . . . schools, church,
home

And then Charlie,
Who had met me once,
Threw his arm around my shoulder
And said,
"This little lady has four kiddies
And a husband to keep in line.
That's all she has time for."

You're lucky, Charlie,
That the "little ladies"
Don't have time to
Straighten you out.

THE AUTOMATED JEWISH MOTHER

The clothes dryer buzzes,
"Come
Hang
Fold
Store
Mend."

I do not respond.

Minutes later
It calls again,
And again
And again
Until I get into my car
To escape.

As I shift into gear
I see
FASTEN YOUR SEAT BELT,
And the car buzzes.

My machines do not force me
To respond to them.
But they make my life miserable
Until I do.

I would destroy them
But I am already
Overrun with guilt.

CLARIFYING MY VALUES

The three of us are having lunch.
My young and beautiful friend
Is asking our opinion.

Should she marry the stable one,
Or have a fling with the exciting one?

My other friend says,
Why not do both.

Why not indeed,
It's quite possible,
Even respectable these days.

In just a minute
She'll ask me what I think.
What am I going to say?

WASH OUT

So, you've given up on your marriage,
Just couldn't take it anymore,
Too many decisions,
Too many problems,
Life was just too complex,
You had to get out,

She's getting older,
And Heavier,
And Menapausal,
And needs more than you can give.

The children are too complicated,
Rude,
Demanding,
And no longer have you on a pedestal,
(You wonder now if they ever did.)

You've found somebody,
Younger,
Simpler,
Who cares only about your needs,
She's made you feel like a man again,
(A young man at that!)

When it came time to play your best hand.
    in this ultimate game,
You opted to start all over again,
From "GO"

Too bad for you,
You missed the part!

IF I HAD A MILLION DOLLARS

One night when we were playing
"If I Had a Million Dollars"
I said,

"If I had a million dollars,
I'd set you up in an apartment
On the intercoastal,
And visit you every Thursday."

You laughed.

But haven't you men been having,
    this fantasy,
About women,
Since time began?

GETTING FREE

I was finally able to meet,
The eminent psychiatrist,
Everyone had been talking
  about,

He shook my hand,
And,
(As I was trying to think of
  something intelligent
  to say)
He said,
"I've read about your husband
  in the papers,
He's quite a guy."

And I said,
"Oh yeah,
Well, I think they should put this
In the headlines,"

CECILY CROSSMAN DID 18 LOADS OF
  WASH THIS WEEK!

Now, why did I say that?

AM I GETTING THROUGH TO YOU?

If I were running things,
I would see that every,
Poor / Black / White / Chicano / Ghetto Dweller /
  Oppressed Person,
Read Pygmalion, (or at least see My Fair
  Lady)

And then require every,
Senator / Mayor / Schoolboard Member / Teacher /
  Commissioner,
To go the other way, (maybe see it backwards?)

Because, this is the truth,
The man cannot deal with what you say,
When he cannot understand what it is you
  are saying.

No kidding, he really doesn't understand!
He lives in another world,
And speaks another language.

LONELY WORLD

Sometimes, when I am crying out
for an,
"I love you,
I need you,
I can't live without you,"
He doesn't deliver.

He just doesn't know what I need.

And then I must accept the fact
once more,
That even the one who knows me best,
Doesn't know me.

THOUGHTS WHILE ATTENDING ONE MORE WORSHIP SERVICE ONE MORE WORKSHOP ONE MORE MEETING WHERE PEOPLE GET TOGETHER TO DISCUSS THE PROBLEM

How many times must we rehearse
our lines,
Before we are allowed to perform
in the show.

THE LADY AND THE GAME

You have let me know that I have
displeased you,
I have not played the game according
to the rules.

Honestly, I have tried,

It is not simply that we are from
different generations,
Or that we are from different
worlds.

We are not even in the same realm
of consciousness.

I do not understand the game,
But if I did,
I am certain, still, that I could
not play.

THE SUPERMARKET

I can't keep my mind on the frozen
    foods,
My thoughts are filled with the horrible
    little man who was peering in
    the window at me,
While I was treating myself to a hot
    fudge sundae at Woolworths.
Why were you looking at me, old man?
Why do you haunt me?
Get out of my mind!

Oh no, there he is again!
He's coming right toward me,
Slowly pushing an empty basket,
With his grimy little hands.
Go away, old man!
Don't you know you disgust me!
Why look at me with those pleading eyes,
Don't you know,
I gave at the office?

Look, what is he doing?
Is he actually putting that package of
    cheese in his pocket?
Come on, old man,
Don't you know that shoplifting is against
    the law?
It's stealing, for heavens sake!
Lucky for you,
I don't want to get involved!

I am so mad!
Seems like I've seen this man before,
In other stores,
In other cities,
It's just not fair,
I have enough things on my mind..
Why do you complicate my life, old man?
What do you want from me?

THE CLASS

He perpetrated his monologue,
While the challenging views of 20
        fertile minds,
Were artfully suppressed,
Being afflicted as he was,
With that malignant academic
disease called,
"Covering the material."

And then,
Like a great mysteriously orchestrated
        "happening,"
The ideas spilled out,
Quickly at first,
With each voice picking up where
        the other left off,
Rejecting, challenging, supporting
Until finally,
The room was so "Electric,"
That even he lit up.

Ah yes, the inmates are taking
        over the asylum,
And it's working!

LAVA

I saw a scientific film
On volcanos.

As the mountain was spewing out
    molten lava,
And the voiceover was explaining
    the cause
In technical jargon
Beyond my comprehension
I thought,

"Wouldn't it be easier
To just toss in a couple of virgins
To calm it down?"

Shocked?
Don't be.

Human sacrifice,
As a simplistic solution
To complex problems
Is still a viable option.

We do it all the time!

PRACTICAL EXISTENTIALISM

John attended the Metropolitan Opera's
Presentation of La Traviata
And spent the entire evening
Fiddling with his tape recorder.

He toured Europe,
And took 37 slides
Of Buckingham Palace alone.

At his wedding,
After doing battle with his priest
Over the matter,
He instructed the photographers
To click away the ceremony.

When his first child was born,
He took notes,
And prepared a booklet
To commemorate the event.

Poor John,
So busy preserving the great moments
of his life,
He missed it.

HELLO SIXTIES

I shouted out the Emancipation
 Proclamation,
The Civil Rights Act,
And the wording to the Equal Rights
 Amendment.

And you said,
"Let's go to bed."

I joined an underground movement,
And plotted to overthrow the government.

And you said,
"You're cute when you're mad."

I blew up your post office,
And half of your university.

And you said,
"Are you having your period?"

With one fell swoop,
I destroyed everything we both held dear,

And you finally said,
"Why are you doing this?"

"I'M JUST TRYING TO GET YOUR ATTENTION!"

THE DEHUMANIZATION OF ALICE

She posed for the number one magazine,
And was euphoric to discover,
That because of her magnificant body
  and brain,
Low and behold!, she made the cover!

Last week I saw Alice on the magazine,
In the midst of a card game on a wooden
  chest,
With the score being kept on her exquisite
  face,
And a beer can sitting on her lovely
  breast.

SPECTATOR SPORT

The judge threw the case out,
Deciding no normal man
Would perpetrate an unprovoked
Sexual attack
On someone he cared about.

She tried to reach him,
That evening
To explain her side
But he was at home
Curled up in bed,
Reading Wallace's
The Fan Club.

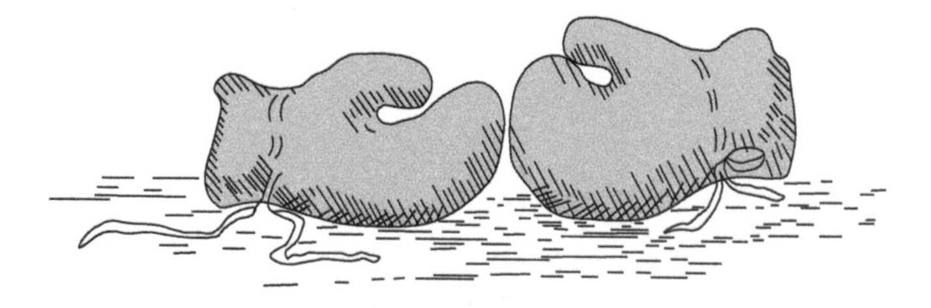

ROCKY

As we left the movie
He said,
"She reminded me of you,
When you used to be,
Shy and small."

And I said,
"What a coincidence!
He reminded me of you
When you were
Dumb and tall!"

IMPROVING OUR IMAGE

I read an article,
In a psychology magazine
Entitled "Why Woman Marry
    Ministers,"
It gave the usual dreary
    reasons,
Until the last one
Which said
"Some women marry ministers
Because as young girls
They have sexual fantasies
About clergymen."

Fantastic!

I can't wait to use that one
The next time somebody asks me.

THE TOTAL ROBOT

For two weeks I agreed with everything you said.
And we both developed ulcers.

I told you the awful speech you made
Was good.
And you said,
"Why did you betray me?"

I stopped wearing pants
And started wearing frilly dresses
And ribbons in my hair.
And you took me to Carvel's for lunch.

I was ready to make love
Every night for two weeks.
And the sixth night
You slept in the car.

I forced Cathy to give away her $25
Overalls.
And you said,
"Why does my daughter hate me?"

I met you at the door
Wearing nothing but my sexy apron,
And you brought home
Three Haitian refugees and a
    Catholic Priest.

I baked you a big apple pie
Every night for a week,
And you said,
"Why aren't you working on your article?"
(Just before you had a gall bladder attack.)

I told the Crisis Center
I couldn't counsel their 12 year old
Victim
Because I had to get my hair done.
And you were ashamed of me.

I said, "Yes, let's"
To everything you suggested.
And our friends had to bail us out of jail.

I dressed all of the children in pink
And lined them up to await your return.
But you never did.

October 5, 1900
Dear Sigmund,
Regarding your recent query,
"What do women want?"
My reply follows.
Everything.
Love,

Cecily

**And now an encore to the original *New Day*.
More poems, either written in or referring to,
the life changing decades of the 60s and 70s.**

THE MYOPIA OF PIOSITY

Spiritual perfection is easy to see.
Just look at me.

DISPAIR

My friend is in love with my husband,
My minister has run off with the choir director,
My analyst is in rehab,
My doctor has a rare disease,
My letter to Dear Abby was returned,
(marked addressee unknown)

Who do I turn to now?

GOODBYE MARTIN

Yesterday we walked with Martin.
It was raining very hard.
Hundreds, thousands pressed against us,
As we neared the college yard.

That morning I had fed my babies,
Dressed them, hugged them with thanksgiving.
Then drove us to our day places
(You know I have to make a living.)

They were all alone in Memphis,
When the awful moment came,
Martin laughing by the railing,
At the small Hotel Lorraine.

People came from everywhere,
Needing rides and food and bed.
We scrambled to fine safe places,
For them to lay their weary heads.

Yesterday we walked with Martin.
It was raining very hard,
Bobby, Ethel, Harry led them,
But hundreds, thousands swarmed the yard.

This morning we made Easter eggs,
For our preschool celebration,
We'll play and sing and clap our hands,
While waiting for the resurrection.

MY OWN WOUNDED KNEE

Neighborhood Conversation Recorded
Exactly as It Took Place

"No, our children don't play with
    guns,
No war games at our house."

"I agree, my Eddie has guns just
    to play cowboys and Indians."

"Well, we just can't justify 'pretend'
    killing people."

"But they aren't real people,
They're Indians."

My first poem published in a literary magazine in 1964.

BUT A PALE SHADOW

Once a man said to me,
I feel the greatest sorrow for those
    people who are rising up from
    the very depths of civilization and
    begging that the world hear their
    agonizing cry.

And I said, "Not I, my friend."
I sorrow for those who have never bothered
    to cry out.

Those who are content to live in mediocrity,
In suspicion of their fellowman,
Never for anything,
Never really against anything.,
Afraid of the outside,
Never knowing the ultimate love which comes
    From giving oneself completely.

Don't look for them in some far away place.
They are all around us.

My heart weeps for them.

And, finally, a poem written by another woman who put into prose her struggles to get free. My mother, Carmen, died in 1947 at the age of 36, after spending several years in a TB sanitarium. I didn't know her well. We visited once a month but were not allowed to be physically close.

But she obviously influenced my life journey.

*****

What goes into this frock that I'm sewing,
Besides a short skirt that leaves panties showing,

And a wee bit of ribbon and buttons and such,
And a small piece of lace - not much.

As I baste it and press it and turn in a seam,
With each careful stitch, I sew in a dream.

- Carmen Strange Riley

*****

Thanks to all of you who continue to fight the good fight.

*****

I was born in Indianapolis, Indiana. My mother died when I was very young so my little brother and I were sometimes farmed out to relatives but we mostly took care of each other.

I'm currently 81 years old. I have four children, ten grandchildren, and one great-grandchild. I've been a ferocious reader all my life and was first introduced to the concept of feminism by Eleanor Roosevelt who wrote a newspaper column long after her husband, President Roosevelt, died.

In 1959 I met my first husband, Ken, and together we dreamed of spending our lives being part of positive change in the world. We married in 1960 and five years later we were off to Atlanta where Ken enrolled in Theology school at Emory University. While there we were caught up in the Civil Rights movement. In 1968 we experienced two significant events. We were part of facilitating the successful integrating of East Lake United Methodist Church and Martin Luther King, Jr. was murdered in Memphis.

We had two toddlers at the time so life was complicated and we didn't really know what our future would look like.

After graduation Ken was an urban minister in South Florida for nine years and later on pastored downtown churches in several Florida cities. Along the way I went to school, wrote and, quite by accident, began a career as a consultant and platform speaker. And we had two more babies.

In the late 1970s and early 1980s, during a time of much unrest, I, along with an African American Episcopal priest, led several workshops on Racism in South Florida. I was later asked to lead a course based on these workshops at the annual statewide meeting of United Methodist Women held at Florida Southern College.

For the next few decades I spoke and led workshops on various topics, always encouraging others to live their best lives. After the Challenger tragedy in 1986, when morale was very low, I was invited to lead a series of workshops, at a sub contracting company at Cape Canaveral.

In 2004, after a decade long illness, that involved dialysis and dementia, Ken died. I cared for him at home during the entire time.

I was happy with all that we accomplished but exhausted. With the children growing their own exciting careers and families, I wanted to reinvent myself.

In 2005, at age 68, I met David. I relaxed for the first time in my life and we had a magical 13 years of extensive travel and enjoying our friends and family and I recorded all of it in my blog "My Best Time" (visit: CecilyCrossman.com).

David died in 2019. And now, even while we are in the midst of a worldwide pandemic, I'm confident that our best days lie ahead.

– Cecily Crossman

I am not throwing away my shot.

- Lin-Manuel Miranda as "Hamilton"

CPSIA information can be obtained
at www.ICGtesting.com
Printed in the USA
LVHW021136240820
664011LV00026B/2223

9 781735 309101